A special thank you
to the sponsors of this book:

Tension Corporation, Sprint Corporation, and Adam & Ashley Rossbach

Published in 2016 by: Spirit Marketing, LLC.
700 Broadway Boulevard, Suite 101, Kansas City, MO 64105
www.HelloSpiritMarketing.com ©2016 Spirit Marketing

All rights reserved. No part of this publication may be reproduced, stored in a retrieval system, or transmitted in any form or by any means (including electronic, mechanical, photocopying, recording, or otherwise) without prior written permission from the publisher.

Major League Baseball trademarks and copyrights are used with permission of Major League Baseball Properties, Inc.

ISBN: 978-1-944953-12-6

Designed in Kansas City, Creative Direction: Chris Evans and Chris Simmons. Written and Illustrated by: Scott Brown.

For information about custom editions, special sales, and premium and corporate purchases, please contact Spirit Marketing at info@hellospiritmail.com or 1.888.288.3972.

Printed 7/16 – 8/16 in USA

Here's a wise owl, his name is Sly,
he loves to read, and wears a bow tie!

He has some pals, one lives in a hut,
there's even a squirrel who carries a nut.

Come see where they live, it's really quite pretty.
This is our home, it's called Kansas City!

The Nelson-Atkins Museum is where we will start, full of paintings, sculptures, and great works of art!

Monet and Rembrandt were painters, you see,
maybe an artist is what you will be!

All kinds of performers touch our hearts,
at the Kauffman Center for the Performing Arts.

When we get hungry, Sly knows what to do...
next stop on our tour – famous KC barbecue!

Pick a good table, and save me a seat.
Try our best sauces, either spicy or sweet.

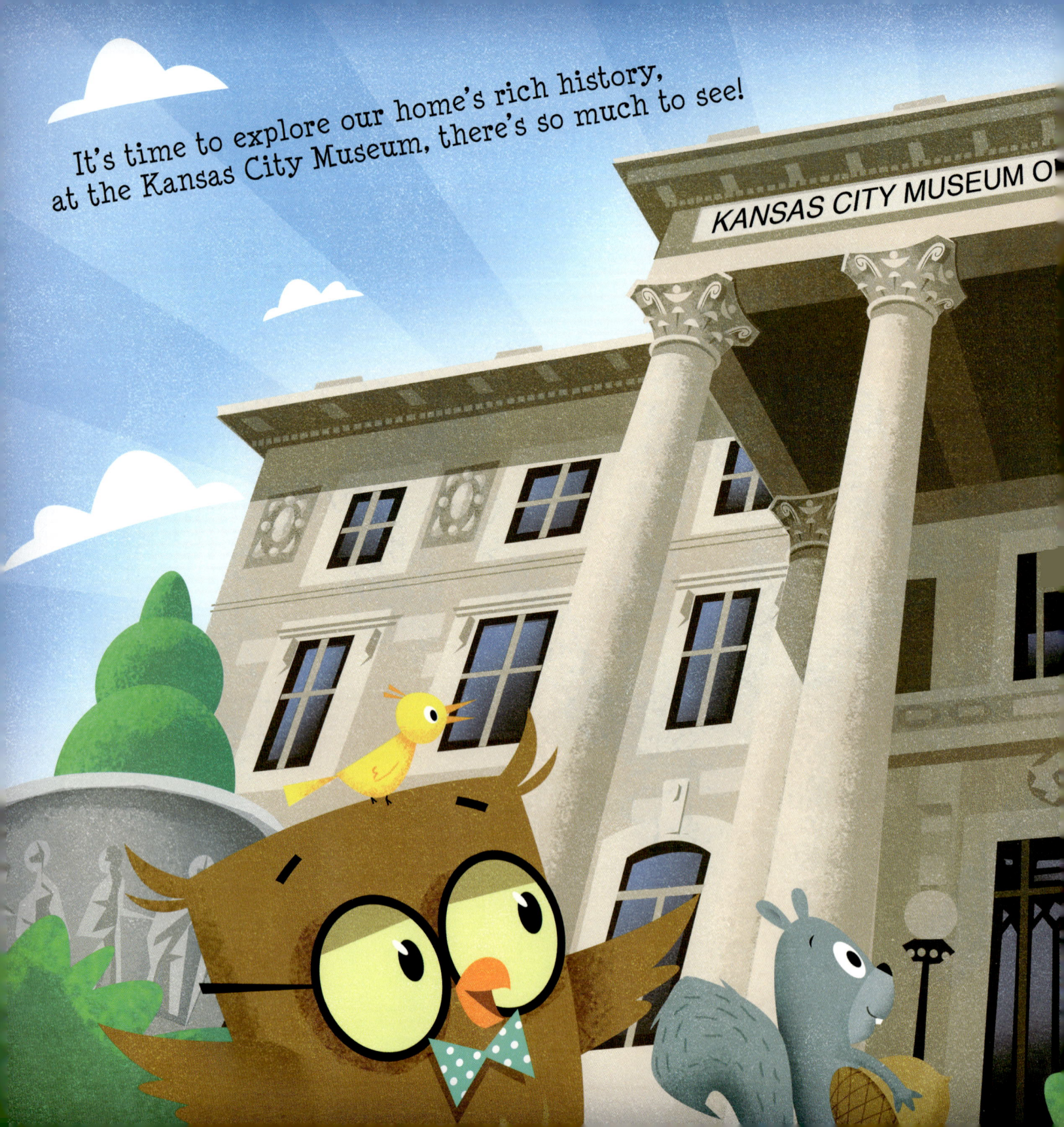
It's time to explore our home's rich history, at the Kansas City Museum, there's so much to see!

It honors the heroes of World War I.
Let's get in line, the tour has begun.

Let's make the Plaza our very next stop,
the streets are all lined with restaurants and shops.

Statues and fountains, they're really quite neat, you can take a cool selfie, or just dip your feet!

The National Museum of Toys and Miniatures is one of a kind,
kids of all ages will have something to find.

Some toys are little, some are tall,
some are really, really small!

A crack of the bat, a loud "hooray!"
here's where the Royals come to play!

Now here is something new to see,
a streetcar that runs for you and me!

From Union Station, where trains often stop,
past Bartle Hall, with art on the top!

Fresh fruits and veggies with dip fill your plate,
there's nothing more fun than a Sporting tailgate!

We eat and play games, right in the lot,
then hurry inside to see Sporting's first shot!

Our friends Sly the Owl, Squirrel and Rabbit, too, all have close cousins that live at the zoo!

Zebras, penguins, and a bat-eared fox, polar bears, meerkats, and snarling crocs!

The KC Library gets funny looks, the front is made out of giant old books!

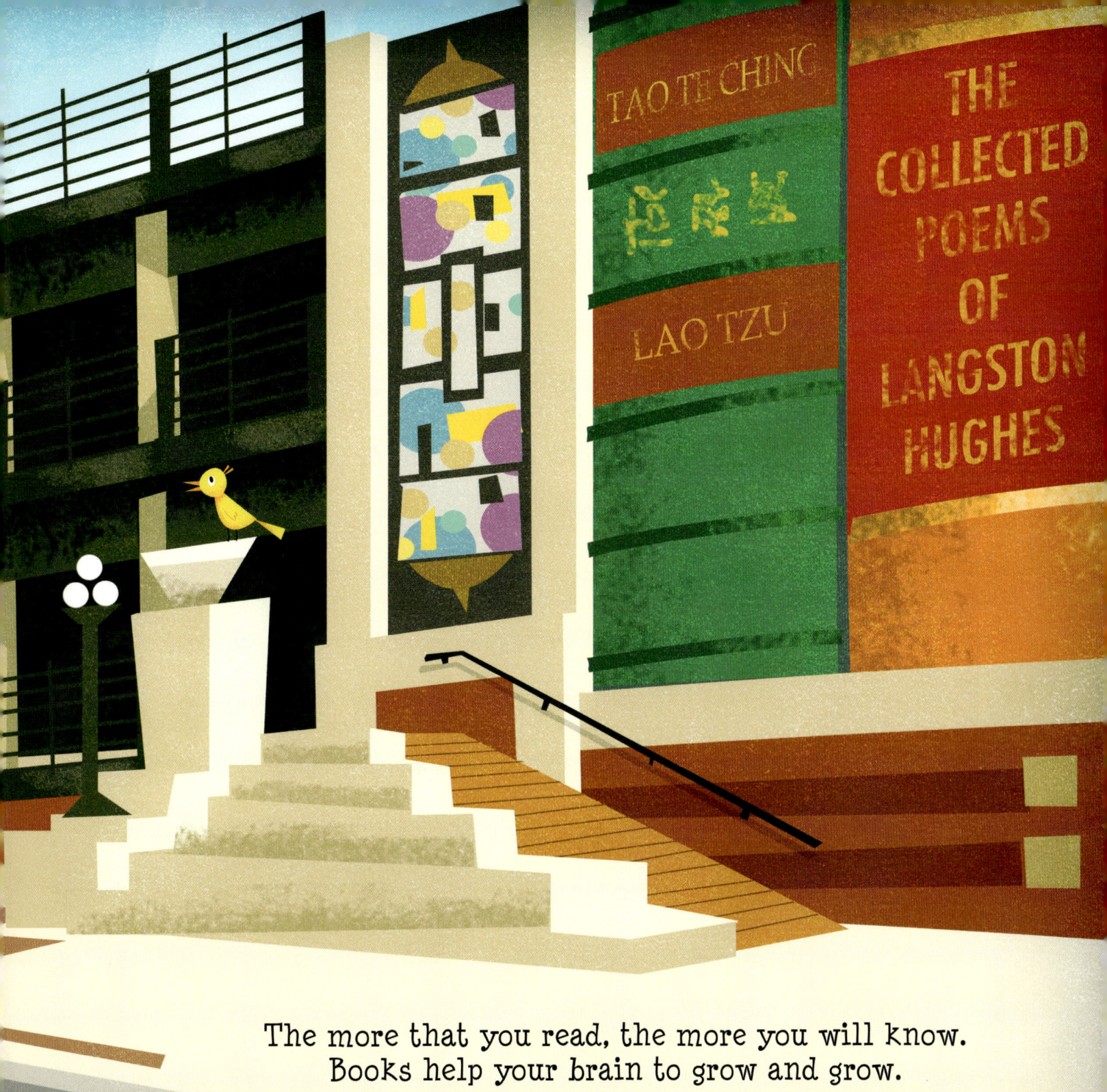

The more that you read, the more you will know.
Books help your brain to grow and grow.

So the journey was all but done.
They sat on a branch and remembered their fun.

Books give you the power to learn and explore.
Read every day, and like Sly, you will soar!

Thank you for supporting elementary reading.

Turn the Page KC supports a positive future for our city by focusing on 3rd grade reading proficiency - a key marker of future success in school and in life.

We work towards this goal by promoting strong school attendance, quality early learning opportunities, participation in summer learning programs, and one-on-one tutoring. You can help ensure that all children have books and volunteers to share them with.

Together, we can make Kansas City the City that Reads.

www.turnthepagekc.org